Amphibiana Leaping GROUND FROGS

by Dawn Bluemel Oldfield

Consultant: Dr. Kenneth L. Krysko
Senior Biological Scientist, Division of Herpetology
Florida Museum of Natural History, University of Florida

BEARPORT PUBLISHING

New York, New York

Credits

Cover and Title Page, © Rene Krekels/Foto Natura/Minden Pictures, © forestpath/Shutterstock, and © prostophoto/Shutterstock; TOC, © Jerry Young/Dorling Kindersley/Getty Images; 4, © Mogens Trolle/ Shutterstock; 5, Courtesy of Dr. Stefan Lötters/Trier University; 6TL, © Audrey Snider-Bell/Shutterstock; 6TR, © age fotostock/SuperStock; 6B, © Gorilla/Shutterstock; 7L, © Daniel Heuclin/NHPA/Photoshot; 7R, © Corbis/ SuperStock; 8, © Art Wolfe/Photo Researchers, Inc.; 9TL, © Joe McDonald/Visuals Unlimited, Inc.; 9TR, © Rolf Nussbaumer/Animals Animals Enterprises; 9B, © Anthony Bannister/NHPA/Photoshot; 10, © Stephen Dalton/ Animals Animals Enterprises; 11, © moodboard/SuperStock; 12, © Tom McHugh/Photo Researchers, Inc.; 13, © Frank Greenaway/Dorling Kindersley/Getty Images; 14, © K. Hinze/Arco Images/Peter Arnold Inc.; 15T, © Nick Garbutt/NHPA/Photoshot; 15B, © George Grall/NGS Image Collection; 16, © Michael Fogden/Animals Animals Enterprises; 17T, © Petra Wegner/Arco Images/Peter Arnold Inc.; 17B, © Joe Holman/Visuals Unlimited, Inc.; 18T, © Gerold & Cynthia Merker/Visuals Unlimited, Inc.; 18B, © Jim Gilbert/Danita Delimont; 19, © José-Luis Gómez de Francisco/Biosphoto/Peter Arnold Inc.; 20T, © Oxford Scientific/(OSF)/Animals Animals Enterprises; 20B, © George Bernard/Photo Researchers, Inc.; 21T, © Wildlife/Peter Arnold Inc.; 21B, © Rene Krekels/Foto Natura/Minden Pictures; 22T, © Thomas Marent/Visuals Unlimited, Inc.; 22B, © Karl Switak/NHPA/Photoshot.

Publisher: Kenn Goin
Editorial Director: Adam Siegel
Creative Director: Spencer Brinker
Design: Debrah Kaiser
Photo Researcher: Omni-Photo Communications, Inc.

Library of Congress Cataloging-in-Publication Data

Bluemel Oldfield, Dawn.
  Leaping ground frogs / by Dawn Bluemel Oldfield ; consultant, Kenneth L. Krysko.
     p. cm. — (Amphibiana)
  Includes bibliographical references and index.
  ISBN-13: 978-1-936087-35-8 (lib. bdg.)
  ISBN-10: 1-936087-35-9 (lib. bdg.)
  1. Frogs—Juvenile literature. I. Title.
  QL668.E2B518 2010
  597.8′9—dc22
                              2009045785

For more information, write to Bearport Publishing Company, Inc., 101 Fifth Avenue, Suite 6R, New York, New York 10003. Printed in the United States of America in North Mankato, Minnesota.

122009
090309CGE

10 9 8 7 6 5 4 3 2 1

Contents

The Longest Leaper

It is a warm, rainy night on the grasslands of southern Africa. A male sharp-nosed grass frog sits near a pond, calling to a female. Suddenly, the frog senses danger. It hears a deadly **mongoose** creeping close by. The hungry **predator** hopes to make the frog its next meal.

△ Mongooses hunt many different animals, including frogs, snakes, mice, and small birds.

In a split second, the frog bursts from the ground and leaps into the tall grass nearby. The hungry mongoose loses sight of the frog—which isn't too surprising. After all, the sharp-nosed grass frog is a difficult animal to catch. Among frogs, it is the best leaper in the world.

A sharp-nosed grass frog named Santjie holds the world record for jumping. In a contest held in 1977, the frog covered a distance of 33 feet 5.5 inches (10.2 m) in three jumps.

△ The sharp-nosed grass frog's powerful back legs are twice the length of its body.

Amazing Amphibians

Like all frogs, the sharp-nosed grass frog belongs to a group of animals called **amphibians**. Toads, salamanders, and newts are also members of this group.

The word *amphibian* means "double life." The name is fitting because most amphibians are at home in two kinds of **habitats**—one in water and one on land.

toad

newt

salamander

There are about 4,000 **species** of frogs in the world. The many different kinds spend their lives in different ways. For example, the sharp-nosed grass frog is one of the many species that lives mostly on land. These frogs are called **terrestrial frogs**, or ground frogs. Other frogs, known as tree frogs, usually live at least a few feet off the ground in trees and other tall plants. Still others, known as **aquatic frogs**, live in water for nearly all their lives.

◁ The goliath frog is an aquatic frog that spends most of its life in water. It is also the biggest frog in the world, growing more than one foot (.3 m) long.

▽ Tree frogs have sticky pads on their toes that help them climb up trees and other plants.

People often think that frogs and toads are two completely different kinds of amphibians. In fact, toads are a kind of ground frog.

toe pads

Places to Call Home

Although ground frogs live mainly on land, they need to stay close to water. Why? The frogs find plenty of insects and other food in and around ponds, lakes, and streams. Water is also a great place to escape from predators on land.

This South American bullfrog has just captured an insect called a walkingstick.

Even when they are out of the water, ground frogs need to keep their skin moist. In fact, if their skin dries out, they will die. Many survive by making their homes in forests, grasslands, and other places where they can find shade and stay out of the hot, drying sun. In these spots, the frogs rest during the day, often under rocks, logs, or fallen leaves. At night, when the air is cooler and more **humid**, they come out to move around and look for food.

Ground frogs live in most parts of the world. This map shows where two kinds—the wood frog and the eastern barking frog—are found.

☐ Where wood frogs live

☐ Where eastern barking frogs live

Many ground frogs **hibernate** to survive the cold of winter. Some find shelter in hollow logs or in spaces between rocks. Others dig shallow winter beds in the ground or under leaves. They rest in these spots until warm weather returns in spring.

An African bullfrog hibernating

Built for Leaping

Many ground frogs are great leapers—jumping to catch food and to escape from danger. These frogs get their leaping ability from their long, powerful back legs. Their strong front legs help them make a smooth landing. The best leapers can make several big jumps in a row.

This photo shows the movement of a ground frog as it leaps through the air.

Some ground frogs cannot make long leaps. Instead, these frogs, known as **burrowing frogs**, are built for digging in the ground. They burrow to make cool, dark, underground spaces where they can keep their skin moist and stay safe from predators. These frogs have shorter legs than leapers do. Burrowing frogs also often have special growths on their feet that act like shovels to help them dig.

Some burrowing frogs live in the desert. They are able to survive by hiding in their burrows during hot, dry times of the year and coming out only after a rainfall.

△ This ground frog, called Spencer's burrowing frog, lives in deserts in Australia.

Fast Food

Ground frogs are not picky eaters. They will eat just about any living creature they can fit into their mouths. Some of their favorite foods are flies, crickets, earthworms, and spiders.

△ An African bullfrog swallowing a mouse

Frogs blink their eyes to help them swallow their food. Blinking causes the frog's eyeballs to sink into its head. The movement helps squeeze the food in the frog's mouth down into its throat.

Many ground frogs use their leaping ability to catch their **prey**. When one of them sees a tasty insect, it springs into action. The frog shoots out its sticky tongue while it is in midair. Then it snatches and pulls its prey into its mouth. Leaping frogs have small teeth that they use for holding on to their prey—but not for chewing. Like all amphibians, they swallow their prey whole.

A ground frog using its tongue to capture prey

Watching Out for Enemies

Ground frogs must protect themselves from predators. Birds, snakes, and lizards are just some of the animals that feast on frogs. Of course, frogs can often leap away from danger. However, they also have other ways to stay safe.

△ **This grass snake has captured a ground frog.**

Frogs have excellent hearing, which helps them know when a predator is near. In addition, a frog's bulging eyes allow it to see in almost every direction. Many frogs also depend on **camouflage** to trick their enemies. The colors and markings on these frogs help them blend in with their surroundings, making them hard to spot.

◁ The long-nosed horned frog is brown and has pointed flaps of skin over its eyes. It easily blends in with dead leaves on the forest floor.

▽ A false-eyed frog showing its eyespots

The false-eyed frog has markings that help scare off enemies. When threatened, the frog puffs out its body and shows two black and white eyespots on its back end. A confused predator thinks that a large, strange creature is staring right at it!

Warning Signs

Some ground frogs do not blend in with their surroundings at all. Their brightly colored skin makes them easy to see. Standing out in this way is also a form of self-defense. How? Most colorful frogs are **poisonous**. Their skin tastes bad and may be deadly. The flashy colors of these amphibians are like a sign that warns, "Stay away!" A predator that has tried to eat one knows that the bright colors mean trouble.

The golden poison frog is one of the most poisonous animals in the world. It has enough poison in its body to kill 10 people!

Brightly colored frogs that are not poisonous are also helped by the way they look. That's because they trick predators. When birds, snakes, and other enemies see the bright warning colors, they pass the frogs by—just like they pass by the ones that really are dangerous.

◁ This ground frog looks like it has paint splashed on its back. Its bright color scares predators away.

The tomato frog is ▷ another frog that uses its color for self-defense.

Eggs in the Water

In the spring, male frogs call, or croak, to attract females. Although they live on land, most ground frogs go to lakes, ponds, or puddles to **mate**. After mating, a female lays her eggs in the water. Like the eggs of all amphibians, they have no shells. Instead, they are covered by a sticky jelly.

△ The male barking frog has a loud call that sounds like "walk! walk!"

Some frogs, such as female barking frogs, do not lay their eggs in the water. Instead, they lay them on moist ground.

A sticky jelly ▷ holds frog eggs together underwater.

Some ground frog species lay only a few eggs—usually in safe, protected places. Others lay hundreds of eggs at a time—usually in places where they are in greater danger of being eaten by fish, birds, and other predators. In these places, only a small number of the eggs will survive and **hatch**.

A ground frog with eggs in a pond

Ready to Live on Land

After about a week, a frog's eggs hatch, and out come little **tadpoles**. The wiggling creatures look more like fish than frogs. Tadpoles have tails but no legs. Like fish, they use **gills** to breathe in **oxygen** from the water.

Tadpoles use their long tails to help them swim.

Over several weeks, ▷ tadpoles grow legs for walking on land.

After several weeks, tadpoles start to grow their back legs. Their gills are replaced with **lungs**, which enable the growing frogs to take in oxygen from air. Within a few months, the tadpoles grow front legs. Their tails shorten and begin to disappear. The little amphibians have turned into froglets, or young frogs. They hop from the water to live on land—just as their parents did.

Frogs don't breathe only through their gills or lungs. Whether they are in water or on land, they also breathe by taking in oxygen through tiny holes in their skin, called pores.

△ Froglets leave the water and live on land. As adults, they will return to the water to mate.

▽ An adult ground frog

Ground Frogs in Danger

Ground frogs have been on Earth for millions of years. However, scientists fear that some species may now be in danger of becoming **extinct** due to diseases and changes in the **environment**.

One of the biggest threats to ground frogs is the loss of their habitat. When people clear land for buildings, crops, or roads, many frogs lose their homes. Frogs are also harmed by pollution.

In some places in the world, certain kinds of ground frogs are already extinct. Here are two kinds that are currently in danger.

Tomato Frog

- This ground frog lives only in the forests of Madagascar, an island off the eastern coast of Africa.
- The frog got its name because its plump, red body looks like a tomato.
- The tomato frog is in danger because the forests where it lives are being cut down. Many frogs have also been taken out of Madagascar to be sold as pets. Selling tomato frogs is now illegal.

California Red-Legged Frog

- The California red-legged frog is one of the largest native frogs in the western United States. It can grow up to five inches (12.7 cm) long.
- California red-legged frogs live near streams in woodlands and grasslands.
- This ground frog is threatened by pollution and by the building of homes and businesses in the places where it lives.

Glossary

amphibians (am-FIB-ee-uhnz) animals that usually spend part of their lives in water and part on land

aquatic frogs (uh-KWAT-ik FROGS) frogs that spend most of their adult lives in water

burrowing frogs (BUR-oh-ing FROGS) frogs that dig holes in the ground in which to live or hide

camouflage (KAM-uh-flahzh) the colors and markings on an animal that help it blend in with its surroundings

environment (en-VYE-ruhn-muhnt) the area where an animal or a plant lives, and all the things, such as weather, that affect that place

extinct (ek-STINGKT) when a kind of plant or animal has died out

gills (GILZ) the body parts of a water animal that are used for breathing

habitats (HAB-uh-*tats*) places in nature where animals are found

hatch (HACH) to come out of an egg

hibernate (HYE-bur-nayt) to spend the winter in a deep sleep to escape the cold

humid (HYOO-mid) slightly wet

lungs (LUHNGZ) the body parts of an animal or a person used for breathing air

mate (MAYT) to come together to produce young

mongoose (MON-gooss) a small, furry animal that lives in Africa and Asia and looks like a ferret or weasel

oxygen (OK-suh-juhn) a colorless gas found in the air and water

poisonous (POI-zuhn-uss) able to kill or harm an animal or a person if eaten

predator (PRED-uh-tur) an animal that hunts other animals for food

prey (PRAY) animals that are hunted by other animals for food

species (SPEE-sheez) groups that animals are divided into, according to similar characteristics

tadpoles (TAD-pohlz) young frogs before they become adults

terrestrial frogs (tuh-RESS-tree-uhl FROGS) frogs that spend most of their adult lives on land

Index

Bibliography

Behler, John L. and Debbie. *Frogs: A Chorus of Colors*. New York: Sterling Publishing (2005).

Beltz, Ellin. *Frogs: Inside Their Remarkable World*. Buffalo, NY: Firefly Books (2005).

Burnie, David, and Don E. Wilson (eds). *Smithsonian Institution: Animal*. New York: DK Publishing (2001).

Read More

Bishop, Nic. *Frogs*. New York: Scholastic (2008).

Kalman, Bobbie. *Frogs and Other Amphibians*. New York: Crabtree Publishing (2005).

Moffett, Mark W. *Face to Face with Frogs*. Washington, D.C.: National Geographic Society (2008).

Learn More Online

To learn more about ground frogs, visit
www.bearportpublishing.com/Amphibiana

About the Author

Dawn Bluemel Oldfield is a freelance writer. In her spare time she enjoys reading, traveling, and working in her yard, which has been designated as a certified wildlife habitat. She and her husband live in Prosper, Texas, just a leap away from Dallas.